OFF-ROADING VEHICLES

DIRT BIKES

TAMRA B. ORR

Mitchell Lane
PUBLISHERS

Parent and Caregiver Tips for Creating Nonfiction Readers

The high-interest topics in the *Off-Roading Vehicles* series are sure to get your young reader excited about reading nonfiction. While exploring a fascinating subject, your reader will be introduced to new concepts, facts, ideas, and vocabulary.

Tips for Reading Nonfiction

Talk about Nonfiction

Explain that nonfiction books provide facts about real-world topics. When readers read nonfiction, they gain a rich understanding of the world. They build background knowledge that provides a foundation for learning and academic success.

Look at the Parts

This book contains the following helpful features. Share the purpose of each feature with your reader.

Photos, Captions, and Graphic Aids
The photos, captions, charts, maps, and other graphic aids in nonfiction texts contain a wealth of information. Help your reader identify different ways information can be displayed. A special feature, "A Closer Look," puts the spotlight on learning through images.

Sidebars
These extra tidbits of information help satisfy readers' curiosity and expand their knowledge.

Table of Contents
Located at the front of the book, this list shows the big ideas within the text and the page numbers where they can be found.

Glossary
Located at the back of the book, the glossary defines key words and phrases that are related to the topic. These words and phrases can be found in the text in **bold** type.

Comprehension Questions (Fact Check)
Multiple-choice questions help readers self-check to make sure they understand what they read.

Index
Located at the back of the book, the index is an alphabetical list of topics and the page numbers where they can be found.

With a little help and guidance, your reader will be on their way to enjoying and learning from nonfiction books.

Mitchell Lane
PUBLISHERS

mitchelllanepub.com

2001 SW 31st Avenue
Hallandale, FL 33009

First Edition, 2026.
Author: Tamra B. Orr
Designer: Kathy Walsh
Editor: Tricia Hoffman

Series: Off-Roading Vehicles
Title: Dirt Bikes / by Tamra B. Orr

Hallandale, FL : Mitchell Lane Publishers, [2026]

Library bound ISBN: 979-8-89260-564-9
Paperback ISBN: 979-8-89260-594-6
eBook ISBN: 979-8-89260-573-1

Photo Credits
Adobe: Background, miloje; Alamy: p16 & 29, Frank Bienewald; p6 & 28, Connect Images; p8 & 28; Ian Shipley; p19 & 29, Michael Doolittle; p5, pbpgalleries; p7, public domain NB/PR; Science Photo Library; p14, ZarkePix; p 17, Volodymyr Melnyk; p11; Kevin J Salisbury via Wiki; Shutterstock: Cover & title pg, Torwaistudio; p24 & 29; Ganstock; p13 & 28; Artur Didyk; p8 The Marinerf 4291; p10, JW Photography; p 112, taelove7; p15, Jacob Lund; p18, PPstock; p21, OlegRi, Allison H. Smith, Andriy Giryak, Sergey Nemirovsky, FernandoV; p22, Sergey Nemirovsky; p25, PPstock; p26, Tonia Kraakman

Contents

Climb On—and Hang On!

Straddle the dirt bike seat.

Check the gas tank.

Flip the kick start lever and listen as the engine comes to life.

Hold on to the handlebars.

Shift into first gear.

Slowly let out the clutch and give the bike a little gas.

After you've done all this, great news—you're ready to ride. Adventure is waiting for you around the next curve or over the next hill. It's go time!

KYLE WILBY
745

From Bicycles to Motorcycles to Dirt Bikes

A dirt bike is a type of motorcycle that is meant to be ridden off-road. A lot is known about dirt bikes, but no one is quite sure who first invented them.

It began with a Frenchman named Pierre Michaux. Pierre was a **blacksmith**. He created the first pedal-driven bicycle in the early 1860s. A few years later, Pierre's son Ernest Michaux added a small steam engine to the bicycle. By the end of the 1800s, the first motorcycles were made in Europe.

Pierre Michaux's pedal-driven bicycle, 1869

The Auto-Bi was the first motorcycle to be widely available in the United States.

BSA Scrambler

Siegfried Bettmann may have invented the first dirt bike. In 1914, he created a sturdy, lightweight, and simple motorcycle that was perfect for off-road adventures. It was called the BSA Scrambler.

In 1948, Soichiro Honda founded the Honda Motor Company. It began producing motorcycles and by 1960, dirt bikes were added. These off-roaders quickly became popular. Other companies, such as Yamaha, Kawasaki, and Suzuki, also began producing them.

Honda

Yamaha

Kawasaki

Growing in Popularity

How popular are dirt bikes? Pretty popular! National races shown on television grabbed people's attention. In 2022, the market for these off-road vehicles in the United States was valued at $4 billion.

Changes in how dirt bikes are made also help increase their popularity. New materials have helped make dirt bikes lighter and tougher. Better **suspension** plus stronger wheels have made them safer for all types of **terrain**. No wonder so many people love these vehicles! They have come a long way since their beginnings.

Alex Harvill

A RECORD BREAKER

The world record for the longest ramp-to-dirt jump is 425 feet (129.5 meters), set by Alex Harvill. That's longer than a football field!

Racing Takes Over

The very first motocross competitions, called scrambles, were held in England in the 1920s. They took place in large meadows or open fields.

In 1948, the first motocross race inside a stadium was held near Paris, France. In the 1950s, dirt bike racing came to the United States. It has grown more and more popular ever since.

WHAT IS MOTOCROSS?

Motocross is a form of off-road motorcycle racing that specifically involves dirt bikes. The indoor version of motocross is called supercross.

Take a Closer Look

Are dirt bikes the same as motorcycles? Yes—and no.

They look similar to motorcycles, but in most states, they do not require any type of license to drive. Why? Because true dirt bikes are not made to go on the road. They belong on trails, paths, and tracks, not streets, sidewalks, or public roads. Only models that have been significantly **modified** are legally allowed on city streets.

A RECOMMENDATION

The American Academy of Pediatrics strongly recommends that children younger than 16 should not ride a dirt bike.

A close look at dirt bikes helps explain why they can't go on streets. They do not have any headlights, brake lights, turn signals, or mirrors. They would be dangerous on the roads!

Instead, dirt bikes are made to climb over tree stumps, scramble across rocks, and dash down dirt forest trails. They are taller than many motorcycles so that they have room to maneuver over bumps and other obstacles.

INTO THE FUTURE

While almost all dirt bikes are gas-powered, electric dirt bikes are growing more popular. They are slower and less powerful, which makes them a good choice for beginners.

Dirt bikes have knobby tires to provide **traction** on loose surfaces like gravel and dirt. They have a long suspension to absorb the impact when riders go over jarring terrain. They are made to push over, past, and across things.

Dirt bike engines range from a beginner's 50 cc (cubic centimeters), which can reach speeds of about 35 to 48 miles (56 to 77 km) per hour, to a professional rider's 500 cc. These bikes can reach speeds of 90 to 110 miles (145 to 177 km) per hour! Thanks to their aluminum frames and wheels, as well as their plastic fenders and panels, most bikes weigh less than 200 pounds (90.7 kg).

IN THE BEGINNING

For young riders, experts recommend beginning with a 50 cc dirt bike as they move very slowly and are low to the ground.

The Right Type

There are several different types of dirt bikes. While most dirt bikes are similar, there are important differences, depending on how they will be used.

Type	Features
Motocross	• One of the most common types of dirt bike • Designed for racing on motocross tracks • Can be used off-road but not on streets • Powerful engine for climbing steep hills
Trail	• One of the most common types of dirt bike • Perfect for beginners • Designed for off-road, **recreational** riding • Made for going longer distances
Enduro	• Built for long-distance endurance rides • Made for distance, speed, and tough terrain • Can be used off-road but not on streets • For advanced riders only
Dual-Sport	• Cross between motocross and enduro bikes • Made for on- and off-road • May include headlights, turn signals, rearview mirrors and other safety essentials for the road
Adventure	• Larger and heavier • Made for on- and off-road • Comfortable seat, extra storage, and a larger gas tank for long-distance adventures

Motocross

Trail

Enduro

Dual-Sport

Adventure

Safety First

No matter what type of dirt bike you ride, or what adventure you take it on, safety has to come first. First, all riders must have a helmet with a chin guard. It should be approved by the U.S. Department of Transportation.

If the helmet doesn't have a face guard, experts recommend wearing goggles. Goggles protect your eyes and face from low-hanging branches, flying rocks, and unexpected road **debris**.

√ Helmet? Check.

√ Goggles? Check.

Now, you can add even more safety gear! Boots that go up over the ankles help protect your feet. Add in knee and shin protectors and a chest guard and you're ready to hit the trails—or the ground if you take a spill.

The Motorcycle Safety Foundation offers DirtBike School, a one-day training course that covers 19 lessons on how to be a safer, better rider. The lessons include tips and skills needed for everything from shifting and turning to counterbalancing and climbing hills.

IN GEAR

The majority of dirt bikes have manual transmissions and rely on three to six **gears** and a clutch to operate.

Your Off-Road Adventure Awaits!

Dirt bikes were made for one thing: adventure! Gear up, get ready, and jump on. Go explore the adventure that awaits around the next curve.

A Closer Look

What is this man doing?

Blacksmiths work to shape and form metal. They use special tools to bend pieces of metal heated over fires. Pierre Michaux and his son used their blacksmithing skills to add pedals to early bicycles.

Who used the first dirt bikes?

The first dirt bikes were called BSA Scramblers. They were put into production in 1914 and were used by soldiers in World War I.

Why is this racer inside?

This race is an example of arenacross. These are fast-paced races that take place indoors, as in this arena.

How did this rider jump so high?

You need the right posture! Experts recommend squeezing the bike with your knees and not leaning too far forward or backward. Your upper body should be kept at a 45-degree angle with your hips.

Why is this rider so small?

Some people begin riding at age three or four! But they have to wait until age 16 to become official dirt bike professionals.

Is this rider actually flying?

No, but it looks like it! This advanced trick is called the Superman Seat Grab. The position of the rider is supposed to mirror the superhero flying in his cape.

Glossary

blacksmith (BLAK-smith)
someone who creates objects by heating and bending iron

clutch (kluhch)
a pedal for controlling a vehicle's gears

debris (duh-BREE)
ruins, rubble, the pieces of something that has been broken or destroyed

modified (MAH-duh-fyd)
changed or altered in some way

suspension (suh-SPEN-shuhn)
a vehicle's springs, shock absorbers, etc.

recreational (rek-ree-AY-shuh-nuhl)
of or relating to recreation, fun, or relaxing activities

terrain (tuh-RAYN)
a section of land

traction (TRAK-shuhn)
the force that keeps a moving object from slipping on a surface

Fact Check

1. The typical dirt bike needs to be _____ in order to go on the street.

   A. modified B. updated C. tested

2. The most important safety equipment for dirt bike riders is a _____.

   A. seat belt B. helmet C. knee guards

3. The first company to produce dirt bikes was _______.

   A. Kawasaki B. Yamaha C. Honda

4. What kind of dirt bike is recommended most for beginners?

   A. enduro B. trail C. adventure

Answers: 1. A, 2. B, 3. C, 4. B

Further Reading

Lanier, Wendy H. *Dirt Bikes (Let's Roll!).* Focus Readers, 2017.

Van, R.L. *Yamaha Dirt Bikes (Dirt Bike Crazy).* North Star Editions, 2019.

Zalewski, Aubrey. *Dirt Bikes (Start Your Engines).* Kaleidoscope Books, 2019.

On the Internet

Dirt Bike Riding for Beginners: The Ultimate Guide
cardosystems.com/blogs/cardo-blog/dirt-bike-riding-for-beginners-the-ultimate-guide
This helpful guide discusses everything from the gear you need to how to start your first dirt bike.

Dirt Bike Riding Techniques for Kids to Master
www.frpmoto.com/blogs/dirt-bike-tips-and-tricks/dirt-bike-riding-techniques-for-kids-to-master
FRP is dedicated to creating "thrilling and confidence riding moments by offering beginner friendly power sports for kids." This site gives guidance on body position, throttle control, and other importing riding skills.

How to Ride a Dirt Bike
www.neighbor.com/storage-blog/how-to-ride-a-dirt-bike/
A guide on how to ride a dirt bike, with a focus on beginner riders.

A Basic Dirt Bike Riding Tips
www.dirtrider.com/basic-dirt-bike-riding-tips/
This article includes tips and inspirational videos from DirtRider.com.

DirtBike School
msf-usa.org/start-your-ride/dirtbike-school/
A one-day training session that covers lessons such as shifting and turning to counterbalancing and climbing hills.

Index

About the Author

Tamra B. Orr is a mom, wife, grandmother, and full-time writer and author living in the beautiful all-terrain Pacific Northwest. She lives in Oregon, close to the site of the Annual Kid's Field Day, a race event for young dirt bike riders held each year. Oregon's varied terrain makes it a favorite spot for many riders. A graduate of Ball State University, Orr has written more than 750 nonfiction and educational books for readers of all ages and absolutely loves her job. It gives her the chance to learn about something new—and then share that information with readers of all ages—every single day.